W9-BUY-377

HOW TO SURVIVE A TORNADO

BY MARNE VENTURA

The Child's World®

Published by The Child's World®
1980 Lookout Drive • Mankato, MN 56003-1705
800-599-READ • www.childsworld.com

Acknowledgments
The Child's World®: Mary Berendes, Publishing Director
Red Line Editorial: Editorial direction and production
The Design Lab: Design
Photographs ©: Clint Spencer/iStockphoto, cover, 1;
Shutterstock Images, 5; Bonnie G. Vculek/Enid News and
Eagle/AP Images, 6; R. Gino Santa Maria/Shutterstock
Images, 9; iStockphoto, 10; Mike Hollingshead/Solent
News/Rex Features/AP Images, 13; Charles Slate/The
Sun News/AP Images, 15; Shae Cardenas/Shutterstock
Images, 16; Eric Vega/iStockphoto, 19

Copyright © 2016 by The Child's World®
All rights reserved. No part of this book may be
reproduced or utilized in any form or by any means
without written permission from the publisher.

ISBN 9781609731618
LCCN 2014959809

Printed in the United States of America
Mankato, MN
July, 2015
PA02260

ABOUT THE AUTHOR

Marne Ventura is the author of more than 20 books for kids. She loves writing about science, technology, health, and crafts. She also contributes stories to children's magazines. Marne lives with her husband on the central coast of California.

TABLE OF CONTENTS

#

Wilma Nelson's **weather radio** turned on. It crackled and woke her up. Then, it sounded a tornado warning. She grabbed her cell phone and glasses and quickly went into her closet. She called for her dog. But it ran away. Nelson had heard a twister might be on its way. She had gathered supplies in the closet before she went to bed.

Nelson heard a sound like an explosion. Her ears hurt. A piece of a wall fell in the closet. It bumped her on the head. She looked up. She could see the sky instead of the ceiling. She tried to stay calm.

As Nelson waited, a tornado swept through her hometown of Woodward, Oklahoma. It was April 15, 2012. The twister stayed on the ground for 37 minutes. It traveled two miles (3 km) and was about 1,300 feet

Tornadoes can happen any time, but most happen during the day.

(400 m) wide. The twister killed six people. It destroyed 100 homes and damaged many others.

Nelson was stuck in the closet after the twister passed. Pieces of **debris** blocked the door. Her neighbors came looking for her. She signaled to them with a

A Woodward resident looks over the damage to Nelson's home.

flashlight. They helped her get out and found her dog safe, too.

Nelson was fortunate to survive the tornado. She is sure her weather radio saved her life.

ENHANCED FUJITA SCALE

Meteorologists measure tornadoes on a scale of 0 to 5. The Enhanced Fujita scale is used to rate how badly a twister damages structures and vegetation. One that blows some shingles off a roof is an EF-0. The worst possible twister is an EF-5. It can destroy an entire house. Scientists use information about how bad the damage is to **estimate** the wind speed of the twister. High wind speeds create the worst damage.

Nelson lives in a region of the United States called Tornado Alley. It has more twisters than any other area. But tornadoes strike all over the earth. They often come without warning. Nelson was ready for the disaster even when she was asleep. She knew the dangers, had a plan, and moved quickly. She knew how to survive a tornado.

CHAPTER TWO

LEARNING THE RISKS

A tornado, or twister, is a tube of rotating wind. It forms underneath a thunderstorm and reaches to the ground. Tornadoes can spin as fast as 300 miles per hour (483 km/h). You cannot see wind. But you can see twisters. They pick up water drops, dust, and other objects. They are strong enough to lift cars and houses.

About 1,000 twisters touch down in the United States each year. This is more than any other country. The storms occur mainly in the central and southern United States. They happen most in the spring between 3:00 p.m. and 9:00 p.m. Most twisters last less than ten minutes. They move across the ground at roughly 30 miles per hour (48 km/h). Twisters usually travel less than 15 miles (24 km) on the ground.

A car lies on its roof after a twister in St. Louis, Missouri, in 2011.

Tornadoes can uproot big trees, which can fall on houses, roads, and power lines.

Twisters can touch down quickly. Sometimes there is little or no warning. A twister surprised the people in Longview, Washington, in October 2014. It ripped the roof off a building. This sent debris flying. Some pieces went through a store's window. Twisters do not happen often in Washington. But the store's employees knew what to do. They hid under desks and tables. No one was hurt.

Falling and flying objects are a big danger when a twister hits. Garage doors and car tires blew through Sweetwater, Texas, during a tornado in 1987.

There are also dangers after a twister. These storms often leave behind dangerous debris, such as broken glass, exposed nails, and splintered wood. The tornado in Sweetwater broke water pipes. It knocked down power and telephone lines. And it threw trees onto roads. This kind of damage can make it hard for people to get around, communicate, and get help. Food spoils quickly without refrigeration. And water from broken pipes is not safe to use.

TORNADO ALLEY

The region from central Texas to South Dakota is called Tornado Alley. These states get warm, moist wind from the Gulf of Mexico in the spring. They also get dry, cold wind from Canada. Warm air usually rises. But here, the warm air from the south gets trapped under the cold air from the north. This causes the warm air to spin. The warm air finally pushes up through the cold. This is an **updraft.** It makes the cold air spin down in a **downdraft.** This makes a twister.

CHAPTER THREE

MAKING A PLAN

Tornadoes can happen quickly. So it is important to learn what to look for ahead of time. The sky might look green or black when a twister is coming. The wind might change direction. Heavy rain or hail might stop suddenly. You might see a funnel-shaped cloud reaching toward the ground. There might be a sound like thunder or a loud jet. Listen to the news if you think a twister is coming. **Officials** will send out information on the radio. A tornado *watch* means you should be ready. A twister might touch down. A tornado *warning* means one has been seen. You should get to a shelter right away if there is a warning.

People who are at home during a twister should go to the lowest level of the building. A cellar or basement

A violent twister touches down in Nebraska in 2011. Tornadoes kill about 60 people each year in the United States.

is best. The next best place is a room on the lowest floor. Stay away from windows. Lie down flat. Protect your head with your arms or a pillow.

Sometimes people are away from home when a twister hits. People who are driving cars should stop, get out, and find the lowest place to wait out the storm. They should lie down in a ditch if no other shelter is around and put their arms around their heads. Overpasses or bridges might seem like safe places to hide under. But they are not. Objects can fly into the tunnel at high speeds and hurt or trap people. Stopping a car under a bridge can also cause traffic accidents and block roads.

DOPPLER RADAR

Scientists use Doppler radar to find and track storms. Radars send radio waves into the sky. Waves run into things like raindrops and clouds and reflect back. The radar can tell how far away the storm is by how long it takes the radio waves to come back. Radio waves react differently to things that move toward and away from them. Doppler radars can pick up on these differences. This allows them to show the movement of storms.

Students practice taking cover at a school in South Carolina in 2014.

A construction worker builds a shelter. Being underground keeps people out of strong winds. It also protects them from flying objects.

Homes in areas where twisters are common often have storm cellars or basements. A twister went through a neighborhood near Moore, Oklahoma, in 1999. It missed Dan Garland's home. But it damaged many homes close by. So he chose to make a storm cellar. Another twister hit the town in May 2013. The Garland family went into the shelter. They waited out the storm. Dan knew building the shelter was a smart choice. When he climbed out of the shelter after the storm, he saw that his house was gone.

Family members who are in different places will want to find one another after a twister. It is important to have a plan. Local phone lines may not work. But sometimes long-distance calls go through. You can call someone who lives out of town on a landline. Family members should pick a person to call and memorize the number. They can leave messages for each other this way. Otherwise, cell phones might work, and texting may work better than calling. You can also pick a meeting place for after the storm.

CHAPTER FOUR

CREATING A KIT

On a normal day, you get water from the kitchen faucet. The refrigerator keeps your food fresh. You turn on the heater if you are cold. Electric lights help you see. Your family can drive you to the doctor if you are hurt.

Houses, hospitals, and grocery stores can be damaged or destroyed in a tornado. Clothing, blankets, and tools can be swept away. Water lines and power lines can snap. Debris can cover roads. It might take days or weeks for workers to repair the damage. Making an emergency kit can help you survive if a tornado turns a normal day into an emergency.

Think about what you and your family will need if caught in a twister. Use the list on the next page to put together a kit. Store your supplies in sturdy, waterproof

Telephone poles block a street in Raleigh, North Carolina, on April 16, 2011. Dozens of twisters struck the state that day.

EMERGENCY KIT CHECKLIST

+ Three gallons (11 L) of water per person

+ Canned and dried food

+ Hand-operated can opener

+ Battery-operated radio with extra batteries

+ Flashlight and extra batteries

+ First-aid kit

+ Moist towelettes, trash bags, and ties

+ Local maps

+ Special medications or eyeglasses

+ Baby or pet supplies

+ Sleeping bags

+ Set of clothing with sturdy shoes for each person

+ Fire extinguisher

bags or buckets with handles. Make sure everyone in your family knows where they are.

Keep your kit in the basement or storm cellar. You can make a second, smaller kit, too. Put water, food, and a first-aid kit in the trunk of your family car. That way, if you are not at home, you will still have what you need.

It might seem like the danger of tornadoes would make people avoid living in places where twisters are common. But many people live in Tornado Alley and other places where the storms are likely to happen. They understand the dangers. But they do not worry. They know that if one does strike, they will be prepared.

PREDICTING A TORNADO

Scientists know what **conditions** must be present for tornadoes to happen. But even when the conditions are right, often tornadoes do not occur. This makes it hard to predict tornadoes. Scientists use computer **models** to help. Computer models use data from radar, weather balloons, satellites, and trained storm spotters to predict when and where a twister will touch down.

Glossary

conditions (kuhn-DISH-uhns) Conditions are things that must happen before something else can occur. Specific air conditions lead to tornadoes.

debris (duh-BREE) Debris are the broken pieces of a building. Wearing sturdy shoes will protect your feet from debris.

downdraft (DOUN-draft) A downdraft is downward-moving air. The updraft and downdraft are both strong in a twister.

estimate (ES-tuh-mate) To estimate is to make a smart guess about the measurement of something. Meteorologists estimate the wind speed of a tornado based on the damage it causes.

meteorologists (mee-tee-uh-RAH-luh-jists) Meteorologists are scientists who study weather. Meteorologists warn people when tornadoes are likely.

models (MAH-duhls) Models are representations that show how something works. Weather models help predict twisters.

officials (uh-FISH-uhls) Officials are people who hold public office. Officials can evacuate residents before a twister.

updraft (UHP-draft) An updraft is upward-moving air. Warm air rises, creating an updraft.

weather radio (WETH-ur RAY-dee-oh) A weather radio is a device able to receive emergency alerts. A weather radio can help people be ready for a twister.

To Learn More

BOOKS

Challoner, Jack. *Eyewitness Hurricane & Tornado*. London: DK, 2014.

Fradin, Judith and Dennis. *Tornado! The Story Behind These Twisting, Turning, Spinning, and Spiraling Storms*. Washington DC: The National Geographic Society, 2011.

Kostigen, Thomas. *Extreme Weather: Surviving Tornadoes, Sandstorms, Hailstorms, Blizzards, Hurricanes, and More!* Washington DC: The National Geographic Society, 2014.

WEB SITES

Visit our Web site for links about surviving a tornado:

childsworld.com/links

Note to Parents, Teachers, and Librarians: We routinely verify our Web links to make sure they are safe and active sites. So encourage your readers to check them out!

Index

LEIGH COUNTY PUBLIC LIBRARIES

FREDERICK COUNTY PUBLIC LIBRARIES

SEP   2016